U0027862

LOVE's BOOK *of* ANSWERS

愛的解答之書

專屬於愛的答案

卡羅·波特
CAROL BOLT

HOW TO USE
LOVE'S BOOK OF ANSWERS

本書使用方法

---

1. 把本書放在腿上或是桌上。

2. 提問問題時，要用「封閉式問題」陳述，並花 10 ～ 15 秒默想。例如：「他喜歡我嗎？」「我是不是該約他出去吃飯？」

3. 詢問時，請放把手放在封面上，並在書緣來回移動。

4. 當你覺得是時候了，按著感動翻開，就是《愛的解答之書》給你的答案。

5. 每問一個問題都要比照此流程。

TRY COMMUNICATING IN AN ENTIRELY NEW WAY

用新的方法溝通看看

ALLOW ROOM FOR SURPRISES

為驚喜留點空間

PASSIONATE INVOLVEMENT WILL BE EXPECTED

———✦———

可以期待激情發生哦！

YOU MAY NEED A NEW PLAN

———◆◆◆———

你可能需要一個新計畫

WHAT WOULD IT DO FOR YOU?

———— •‡• ————

這麼做對你有啥好處？

EMPHASIZE PARTICIPATION

有參與才是重點

DON'T TRY TOO HARD

———◆◆———

別太用力

YOU'LL BE MISERABLE
IF YOU SETTLE

——— ·•· ———

現在妥協，將來傷悲

YOU'VE GOT ALL THE RIGHT MOVES

———— •••• ————

你現在做的事都對

NOT SO FAST; MAKE IT LAST

———•••———

別這麼快，細水長流比較重要

YOU'VE GOT WHAT IT TAKES

———◆◆◆———

該有的你都有了

A HEADACHE COULD BE ADVANTAGEOUS

---◆◆---

是件麻煩事，但搞不好會有幫助

SHOW 'EM WHAT YOU'RE MADE OF

———◆◆◆———

讓他們看看你多有料

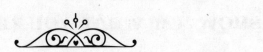

WATCH OUT FOR CLINGING VINES

———•••———

小心，水蛭出沒請注意！

KEEP YOUR OPTIONS OPEN

———◆◆———

多為自已留點選擇

TELL SOMEONE ALL ABOUT IT

---◆◆◆---

找個人聊聊

IS IT SOMETHING YOU'LL WANT AGAIN...AND AGAIN?

這是件你一直想要的事嗎？

PLAY IT CLOSE TO THE HEART

---•••---

感覺的事，不用跟別人多說

THE OUTCOME COULD BE GOLDEN

———◆◆◆———

結果或許會很不錯哦！

CALL NOW

———••———

電話現在就給它打過去

DON'T SPEND TOO MUCH TIME TALKING ABOUT IT

———◆◆◆———

別花太多時間談論這件事

DON'T CENSOR YOURSELF

——◆◆——

別對自己這麼吹毛求疵

EXPECT SOMETHING BIG

———◆◆◆———

期待接下來的大事

IT'S FOR REAL

———•••———

要來真的了喔！

RELAX

放～輕～鬆

DON'T SPEND A LOT OF TIME THINKING ABOUT IT

---◆◆◆---

別花這麼多時間想這件事

KISS NOW, TALK LATER

———◆◆◆———

要聊之後再聊，現在先給他親下去！

GET STRAIGHT TO THE POINT

---◆◆---

直搗黃龍！

KEEP IT TO YOURSELF

---•••---

這事你自己知道就好了

BE A GOOD FRIEND

——— •••• ———

當他的好朋友

YOU MAY HAVE TO COMPROMISE

---◆◆---

你可能得退一步

CELEBRATE THEIR QUIRKINESS

---◆◆◆---

為他們的古怪喝采

ASK FOR MORE

去多要一些

ALMOST, BUT NOT JUST YET

———•••———

快了，但再等等

TALK NOW; KISS LATER

————◆◆◆————

要親之後再親，現在先好好聊聊！

KEEP YOUR FEET ON THE GROUND

———◆◆———

腳踏實地一點吧！

DON'T BE COY

———◆◆———

别太忸怩作態

MIGHT BE TIME TO SEND THEM SOME FLOWERS

---◆◆◆---

該是送些花的時候了

SHOW THEM THAT YOUR HEART IS IN IT

———— •♦• ————

讓他們知道你很感興趣

INVITE THEM ON THE PERFECT ADVENTURE

———— •••• ————

邀請他們一起加入這場完美冒險

YES

——•••——

好啊！！！！

DON'T GET MIXED UP IN IT

———◆◆◆———

別去蹚這渾水

MAKE A GAME OF IT

———— •••• ————

讓它成為一場遊戲吧！

DON'T BE TOO SENTIMENTAL

———◆◆◆———

别太多愁善感

IT'S BOUND TO LAST

———— •••• ————

此情註定可長久

WAIT A BIT

———◆◆◆———

再等一下……………………

YOU AREN'T THE ONLY ONE
WHO IS NERVOUS

---◆◆◆---

緊張的不只你一個

IF YOU'RE IN HOT WATER;
IT'S BEST TO MAKE BUBBLES

---◆◆◆---

水深火熱中？泡澡正合適！

DO WHAT YOU'RE TOLD

———◆◆———

按照別人的建議做吧！

TELL 'EM WHAT YOU WANT

———•••———

把你想要的告訴對方

ROMANCE YOUR WAY INTO IT

———•••———

浪漫地搞定它吧！

YOU MAY FIND IT DIFFICULT TO RESIST

———•••———

很難抗拒，對吧！

MAKE A COMMITMENT

————◆◆◆————

做出承諾吧！

EXPAND YOUR VIEW OF PLEASURE

———•••———

放寬對「樂子」的定義吧！

THE MORE, THE MERRIER

———•••———

越多越開心

IT'S ALL FOREPLAY

———•••———

這只是開胃菜而已

BE CLEAR ABOUT WHAT YOU WANT

———◆◆◆———

搞清楚自己想要什麼

BE PERSISTENT

———◆◆◆———

堅持下去

INDULGE YOUR APPETITES

---◆◆◆---

放縱一下又何妨？

START SOMETHING NEW

---◆◆◆---

試些新招吧！

PUSH A LITTLE HARDER

———— •••• ————

再努力試試

HOLD ON

———◆◆———

齁住啊～～～！！！

CHARM YOUR WAY INTO IT

———◆◆◆———

運用你的魅力吧！

DON'T KEEP ANY SECRETS

———◆◆———

不要再保密了

IT'LL BE A GREAT ADVENTURE

———•••———

會是場棒呆了的冒險

ONLY BITE OFF WHAT YOU CAN CHEW

肚子有多大，嘴巴吃多少

FOR NOW, KEEP IT TO YOURSELF

———•••———

暫時先別跟人說

WAIT UNTIL YOU'RE ASKED

有人問了再行動

ASK THEM OUT ON A DATE

———◆◆◆———

問對方要不要來場約會

SET SOME GROUND RULES

---•••---

訂定一些基本原則

USE YOUR IMAGINATION

———◆◆◆———

運用你的想像力

BE BOLD

———◆◆◆———

大膽一點！

IT'S UP TO YOU

———•••———

由你決定！

FLIRT, FLIRT, FLIRT

---◆◆◆---

調情、調情、調情，很重要所以說三遍

DON'T WAIT TOO LONG

———— ◆◆◆ ————

別等太久

ALL THE BEST THINGS ARE SEEKING YOU OUT

————— •‡• —————

所有美好的事物都已經出門找你

A NEW STYLE COULD BE JUST WHAT YOU NEED

---◆◆◆---

或許你現在就是需要走個新路線

COULD IT BE JUST A PHASE?

會不會只是個過程？

THERE MAY BE OTHERS TO CONSIDER

———— •••• ————

或許可以考慮其他人？

GIDDYUP!

———✦———

衝啊！！！！！！！

MODEST MOVES LAST LONGER

———◆◆◆———

中庸之舉才能持續得久

IT COULD PROVE TO BE
IRRESISTABLE

---◆◆◆---

就跟你說很難拒絕了吧！

DON'T PACK YOUR BAGS YET

———— ◆◆◆ ————

還不到打包回家的時候！

REINVENT A FANTASY

———•••———

再創一個新幻想

IT'S GONNA BE SWEET

———◆◆◆———

這會很甜蜜的

IT COULD BE HARD,
BUT THAT'S NOT ALL BAD

---◆◆◆---

可能不容易，但也不是真的這麼糟啦！

THE DIFFERENCES COULD
BE THRILLING

———— ••• ————

差別會大到讓你合不攏嘴

TAKE YOUR TIME;
YOU'LL WANT THIS TO LAST

---◆◆◆---

慢慢來，你會希望可以長久

WORK IT OUT

————◆◆————

想辦法解決

IT'LL BE WORTH IT

————•••————

會值得的

NEGOTIATE A FRESH START

———•••———

談看看能否重新開始

IT'S PROBABLY NOT A
CASUAL THING

— ••• —

這可能不是件隨興為之的事

KNOW WHEN IT'S TIME TO GO

—◆◆◆—

要知道何時該走人

KEEP YOUR HEART IN CHECK

---◆◆◆---

別太隨心所欲

THERE MAY BE NO LOGICAL EXPLANATION FOR IT

———•••———

這件事大概沒有什麼合理的解釋

SLEEP ON IT

———•••———

好好考慮再做決定

SET A DATE

———◆◆———

訂下一個日期

DON'T WAIT TO BE SEDUCED

---◆◆◆---

別只是等人來撩

IT'S TIME TO GO

該是閃人的時候了

MAKE THE MOST OF IT

———◆◆◆———

善加利用

DON'T TAKE IT TOO SERIOUSLY

---◆◆◆---

別太認真了

IT'S NOT WHAT YOU THINK

——◆◆◆——

不是你想的那樣

YOU MIGHT NEED A LITTLE SPACE

———◆◆◆———

你可能需要一些空間

MAYBE TOMORROW

———•••———

明天再說吧！

WHAT ARE YOU WAITING FOR?

———— ••• ————

你還在等什麼？

FULL STEAM AHEAD

———◆◆◆———

全速前進！！！！

THE WAY TO BE SURE,
IS TO GET CLOSER

----- ••• -----

要確定只有一個辦法：再靠近一點吧！

MAKE ROOM FOR IT

———◆◆◆———

為此事保留點空間

KEEP IT LIGHT AND EASY

---◆◆---

輕鬆、簡單以對

YOU COULD BE IN OVER YOUR HEAD

你可能會陷入麻煩難以脫身

RUB TWO THINGS TOGETHER, SEE IF YOU CAN START A FIRE

靠近一點，看能否撞出火花

START BY BUILDING A NEST

———◆◆◆———

首先，先把你的豬窩整理好！

ONCE YOU'RE COMMITTED, DON'T HESITATE

———•••———

一旦定下來以後就別想東想西了

STEERING TOWARDS ADVENTURE, WILL KEEP THINGS INTERESTING

———◆◆———

朝冒險前進，事情就會有趣

IS IT WHAT YOU WANT?

———◆◆◆———

這真的是你想要的嗎？

TOO MUCH CAUTION WON'T LEAD TO HAPPINESS

———••———

過多顧慮，幸福飛去

FIND OUT MORE ABOUT IT

——— •◦• ———

找出更多相關訊息

LOVE THE ONE YOU'RE WITH

好好愛你身邊的那個他

IT COULD LEAVE YOU BORED

——•••——

你可能會覺得很無聊

ALLOW THE ANTICIPATION TO SIMMER

—◆◆—

讓期待慢慢發酵

TRY EVERYTHING,
BUT NOTHING TO EXCESS

———•••———

什麼方法都可試，但小心別做過頭了

WAIT FOR ANOTHER OFFER

---◆◆◆---

等待看看有無其他選擇

IT WILL BE THE BEST SO FAR

——•••——

是目前為止最好的選項了

BE READY TO MOVE QUICKLY

———◆◆———

準備好快速行動

RECONSIDER YOUR APPROACH

---◆◆◆---

這方法要再想想

THERE IS NO NEED TO WORRY

———◆◆———

免煩惱！

YOU WILL GET THE CHANCE

———— ••• ————

你會有機會的

CHANGE WOULD BE GOOD FOR YOU

改變對你是件好事

LAUGH ABOUT IT

———◆◆◆———

笑一笑讓它過去吧！

DON'T TRY TOO HARD TO MAKE IT HAPPEN

———•••———

別為了達到目的不擇手段

YOU ARE VERY MUCH FAVORED

---◆◆◆---

老天非常眷顧你

ARE YOU READY?

你準備好了嗎？

THE RESULTS ARE SWEET

———◆◆———

結果會是甜美的

WHAT YOU CHOOSE WILL HAVE LONG LASTING EFFECTS

————— •••• —————

你的選擇會帶來長遠影響

THE BEST IS YET TO COME

————◆◆————

最棒的事還在後頭呢！

IT WILL TRANSFORM YOU

———◆◆◆———

這會讓你脫胎換骨

DON'T LOSE YOURSELF IN IT

———— ••• ————

别迷失其中哪！

A LITTLE SKEPTICISM WILL BE HEALTHY

———— •••• ————

些許（適量的）疑神疑鬼有益身心健康

YOU WILL BENEFIT FROM
WHATEVER HAPPENS

——— ••• ———

不論發生什麼，都對你有益

LET IT UNFOLD NATURALLY

———◆◆———

讓它自然而然發生吧！

THE CLOSER YOU BECOME,
THE MORE COMFORTABLE YOU
SHOULD FEEL

———◆◆———

你們越親密，你就該越自在

OFFER SOME ENCOURAGEMENT

鼓勵對方一下吧！

LET IT COME TO YOU

———◆◆———

守株待兔！

BECOME WHAT YOU SEEK

—— ◆◆◆ ——

不管你在找尋什麼，先讓自己成為那樣的人吧！

LOVE MAY ARRIVE IN A
SURPRISE PACKAGE

—–•••—–

愛情會像驚喜一樣來到

DON'T LET YOUR CONFIDENCE BE RUFFLED

———•••———

別讓你的自信被擾亂

IT'LL TAKE A LITTLE COURAGE

—◆—

你需要鼓起一點勇氣

YOU WOULD BE DIFFICULT
TO RESIST

———•••———

你會讓人很難抗拒哦！

IT MIGHT BE HARD, BUT MOST VALUABLE THINGS ARE

———◆◆◆———

可能很困難，但珍貴事物向來難得

TAKE THE TIME TO LET IT GROW

———•••———

花時間培養感情

THERE'S SO MUCH TO BE OPTIMISTIC ABOUT!

––––––•••––––––

值得樂觀以對的事還多著的呢！

BE APPRECIATIVE OF ANOTHER POINT OF VIEW

---◆◆◆---

別人有不同的觀點？值得感恩！

DON'T CHANGE A THING

———— •••• ————

啥都不用改！你這樣就很好

TRY MORE SPONTANEITY

———◆◆———

試著再順其自然一點吧！

BECOME YOUR FANTASY

---◆◆---

成為你幻想中的樣子！

LISTEN FOR THE BEST
OPPORTUNITY

———◆◆◆———

用心聽，最好的機會要來了！

CREATE A NEW WAY TO EXPERIENCE IT

———•+•———

用創新的方式感受吧！

SOMETIMES LOVE CAN BE MESSY

---◆◆◆---

有時愛情就是一團亂嘛！

MAKE TIME FOR THEM

—◆◆—

撥出時間給對方

CREATE SOMETHING NEW TOGETHER

———— •••• ————

一起玩出新創意

SHARE A COMPLIMENT WITH THEM

———•••———

稱讚一下對方吧！

MAKE THE EFFORT TO
HAVE MORE FUN

———•••———

用力找樂子

SAY 'YES'

———◆◆◆———

說「我願意」

YOU MIGHT NEED TO MAKE MORE TIME TO PLAY!

———•••———

你可能需要多撥出時間去玩樂

ASK WHAT MAKES THEM HAPPY, THEN DO THAT

———— •‧• ————

問對方什麼事會讓他開心，然後就去做吧！

MAKE THE FIRST MOVE

———◆◆◆———

你先主動出擊

ACKNOWLEDGE THE
PRACTICAL PARTS

你得承認，某部分是滿有建設性的

TALK IT OUT

---••---

去把事情談開吧！

TRY COMMUNICATING IN AN ENTIRELY NEW WAY

————— •••• —————

用新的方法溝通看看

ALLOW ROOM FOR SURPRISES

為驚喜留點空間

PASSIONATE INVOLVEMENT WILL BE EXPECTED

———— ••• ————

可以期待激情發生哦！

YOU MAY NEED A NEW PLAN

---◆◆◆---

你可能需要一個新計畫

WHAT WOULD IT DO FOR YOU?

---◆◆◆---

這麼做對你有啥好處？

EMPHASIZE PARTICIPATION

---◆◆---

有參與才是重點

DON'T TRY TOO HARD

———— •••• ————

別太用力

YOU'LL BE MISERABLE IF YOU SETTLE

————•••————

現在妥協，將來傷悲

YOU'VE GOT ALL THE RIGHT MOVES

---•••---

你現在做的事都對

NOT SO FAST; MAKE IT LAST

別這麼快，細水長流比較重要

YOU'VE GOT WHAT IT TAKES

———◆◆◆———

該有的你都有了

A HEADACHE COULD BE ADVANTAGEOUS

————◆◆————

是件麻煩事，但搞不好會有幫助

SHOW 'EM WHAT YOU'RE MADE OF

— ••• —

讓他們看看你多有料

WATCH OUT FOR CLINGING VINES

---•••---

小心，水蛭出沒請注意！

KEEP YOUR OPTIONS OPEN

———◆◆———

多為自己留點選擇

TELL SOMEONE ALL ABOUT IT

————•••————

找個人聊聊

IS IT SOMETHING YOU'LL WANT
AGAIN...AND AGAIN?

———◆◆◆———

這是件你一直想要的事嗎?

PLAY IT CLOSE TO THE HEART

---◆◆◆---

感覺的事，不用跟別人多說

THE OUTCOME COULD BE GOLDEN

---◆◆◆---

結果或許會很不錯哦！

CALL NOW

---◆◆◆---

電話現在就給它打過去

DON'T SPEND TOO MUCH TIME TALKING ABOUT IT

----◆◆◆----

別花太多時間談論這件事

DON'T CENSOR YOURSELF

———•••———

別對自己這麼吹毛求疵

EXPECT SOMETHING BIG

———— ✦ ————

期待接下來的大事

IT'S FOR REAL

———— ••• ————

要來真的了喔！

RELAX

———◆◆———

放～輕～鬆

DON'T SPEND A LOT OF TIME THINKING ABOUT IT

———•••———

別花這麼多時間想這件事

KISS NOW, TALK LATER

———— ••• ————

要聊之後再聊，現在先給他親下去！

GET STRAIGHT TO THE POINT

———◆◆◆———

直搗黃龍！

KEEP IT TO YOURSELF

---◆◆◆---

這事你自己知道就好了

BE A GOOD FRIEND

當他的好朋友

YOU MAY HAVE TO COMPROMISE

—◆◆◆—

你可能得退一步

CELEBRATE THEIR QUIRKINESS

———◆◆———

為他們的古怪喝采

ASK FOR MORE

———◆◆———

去多要一些

ALMOST, BUT NOT JUST YET

———◆◆◆———

快了，但再等等

TALK NOW; KISS LATER

---◆◆---

要親之後再親，現在先好好聊聊！

KEEP YOUR FEET ON THE GROUND

---◆◆◆---

腳踏實地一點吧！

DON'T BE COY

— ◆◆◆ —

别太忸怩作态

MIGHT BE TIME TO SEND THEM SOME FLOWERS

—— ••• ——

該是送些花的時候了

SHOW THEM THAT YOUR HEART IS IN IT

———— •••• ————

讓他們知道你很感興趣

INVITE THEM ON THE PERFECT ADVENTURE

—— ✦ ——

邀請他們一起加入這場完美冒險

YES

好啊！！！！

DON'T GET MIXED UP IN IT

———◆◆◆———

別去蹚這渾水

MAKE A GAME OF IT

———◆◆◆———

讓它成為一場遊戲吧！

DON'T BE TOO SENTIMENTAL

———•••———

别太多愁善感

IT'S BOUND TO LAST

此情註定可長久

WAIT A BIT

—◆◆◆—

再等一下‧‧‧‧‧‧‧‧‧‧‧‧‧‧‧‧‧‧‧‧‧

YOU AREN'T THE ONLY ONE
WHO IS NERVOUS

———— ••• ————

緊張的不只你一個

IF YOU'RE IN HOT WATER;
IT'S BEST TO MAKE BUBBLES

---◆◆◆---

水深火熱中？泡澡正合適！

DO WHAT YOU'RE TOLD

———•••———

按照別人的建議做吧！

TELL 'EM WHAT YOU WANT

——— •••• ———

把你想要的告訴對方

ROMANCE YOUR WAY INTO IT

———◆◆◆———

浪漫地搞定它吧！

YOU MAY FIND IT DIFFICULT TO RESIST

---•••---

很難抗拒，對吧！

MAKE A COMMITMENT

———•••———

做出承諾吧！

EXPAND YOUR VIEW OF PLEASURE

———◆◆◆———

放寬對「樂子」的定義吧！

THE MORE, THE MERRIER

—◆—

越多越開心

IT'S ALL FOREPLAY

————•••————

這只是開胃菜而已

BE CLEAR ABOUT WHAT YOU WANT

———◆◆———

搞清楚自己想要什麼

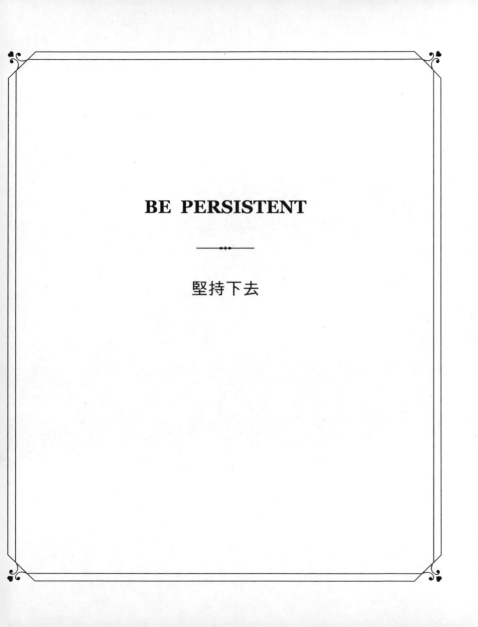

BE PERSISTENT

———◆◆◆———

堅持下去

INDULGE YOUR APPETITES

———◆◆◆———

放縱一下又何妨？

START SOMETHING NEW

———— ••• ————

試些新招吧！

PUSH A LITTLE HARDER

---•••---

再努力試試

HOLD ON

———— ✦ ————

觔住啊～～～！！！

CHARM YOUR WAY INTO IT

———◆◆◆———

運用你的魅力吧！

DON'T KEEP ANY SECRETS

———◆◆◆———

不要再保密了

IT'LL BE A GREAT ADVENTURE

———— •••• ————

會是場棒呆了的冒險

ONLY BITE OFF WHAT YOU CAN CHEW

—◆◆◆—

肚子有多大，嘴巴吃多少

FOR NOW, KEEP IT TO YOURSELF

暫時先別跟人說

WAIT UNTIL YOU'RE ASKED

———◆◆◆———

有人問了再行動

ASK THEM OUT ON A DATE

———— ✦ ————

問對方要不要來場約會

SET SOME GROUND RULES

———◆◆◆———

訂定一些基本原則

USE YOUR IMAGINATION

———•••———

運用你的想像力

BE BOLD

————— ◆◆◆ —————

大膽一點！

IT'S UP TO YOU

———•••———

由你決定！

FLIRT, FLIRT, FLIRT

———◆◆———

調情、調情、調情，很重要所以說三遍

DON'T WAIT TOO LONG

———◆◆◆———

別等太久

ALL THE BEST THINGS ARE
SEEKING YOU OUT

———— •••• ————

所有美好的事物都已經出門找你

A NEW STYLE COULD BE JUST WHAT YOU NEED

———◆◆◆———

或許你現在就是需要走個新路線

COULD IT BE JUST A PHASE?

———◆◆◆———

會不會只是個過程？

THERE MAY BE OTHERS
TO CONSIDER

---◆◆◆---

或許可以考慮其他人？

GIDDYUP!

———◆◆———

衝啊！！！！！！！

MODEST MOVES LAST LONGER

———— •••• ————

中庸之舉才能持續得久

IT COULD PROVE TO BE
IRRESISTABLE

———•••———

就跟你說很難拒絕了吧！

DON'T PACK YOUR BAGS YET

———— •••• ————

還不到打包回家的時候！

REINVENT A FANTASY

———•••———

再創一個新幻想

IT'S GONNA BE SWEET

---◆◆---

這會很甜蜜的

IT COULD BE HARD,
BUT THAT'S NOT ALL BAD

可能不容易，但也不是真的這麼糟啦！

THE DIFFERENCES COULD BE THRILLING

———•••———

差別會大到讓你合不攏嘴

TAKE YOUR TIME;
YOU'LL WANT THIS TO LAST

———◆◆◆———

慢慢來，你會希望可以長久

WORK IT OUT

———◆◆◆———

想辦法解決

IT'LL BE WORTH IT

——◆◆——

會值得的

NEGOTIATE A FRESH START

---•••---

談看看能否重新開始

IT'S PROBABLY NOT A CASUAL THING

———•••———

這可能不是件隨興為之的事

KNOW WHEN IT'S TIME TO GO

———•••———

要知道何時該走人

KEEP YOUR HEART IN CHECK

別太隨心所欲

THERE MAY BE NO LOGICAL EXPLANATION FOR IT

———◆◆◆———

這件事大概沒有什麼合理的解釋

SLEEP ON IT

———◆◆———

好好考慮再做決定

SET A DATE

———✦✦———

訂下一個日期

DON'T WAIT TO BE SEDUCED

---◆◆◆---

別只是等人來撩

IT'S TIME TO GO

———◆◆◆———

該是閃人的時候了

MAKE THE MOST OF IT

———◆◆◆———

善加利用

DON'T TAKE IT TOO SERIOUSLY

———◆◆◆———

別太認真了

IT'S NOT WHAT YOU THINK

不是你想的那樣

YOU MIGHT NEED A LITTLE SPACE

你可能需要一些空間

MAYBE TOMORROW

---•••---

明天再說吧！

WHAT ARE YOU WAITING FOR?

你還在等什麼？

FULL STEAM AHEAD

———◆◆◆———

全速前進！！！！

THE WAY TO BE SURE,
IS TO GET CLOSER

———◆◆◆———

要確定只有一個辦法：再靠近一點吧！

MAKE ROOM FOR IT

———◆◆———

為此事保留點空間

KEEP IT LIGHT AND EASY

———◆◆◆———

輕鬆、簡單以對

YOU COULD BE IN OVER YOUR HEAD

---◆◆◆---

你可能會陷入麻煩難以脫身

RUB TWO THINGS TOGETHER, SEE IF YOU CAN START A FIRE

靠近一點，看能否撞出火花

START BY BUILDING A NEST

—◆◆◆—

首先，先把你的豬窩整理好！

ONCE YOU'RE COMMITTED, DON'T HESITATE

---◆◆◆---

一旦定下來以後就別想東想西了

STEERING TOWARDS ADVENTURE, WILL KEEP THINGS INTERESTING

朝冒險前進，事情就會有趣

IS IT WHAT YOU WANT?

———•••———

這真的是你想要的嗎？

TOO MUCH CAUTION WON'T LEAD TO HAPPINESS

過多顧慮，幸福飛去

FIND OUT MORE ABOUT IT

---•••---

找出更多相關訊息

LOVE THE ONE YOU'RE WITH

————◆◆◆————

好好愛你身邊的那個他

國家圖書館出版品預行編目資料

愛的解答之書：專屬於愛的答案 / 卡羅・波特
（Carol Bolt）著；念念譯. -- 臺北市：三采文化，
2019.01
面；　公分. --（Mindmap180）
譯自：Love's book of answers

ISBN：978-957-658-123-6（平裝）
1. 戀愛 2. 生活指導

544.37　　　　　　　　　　　　107023930

suncolor
三采文化集團

Mind Map 180

愛的解答之書
專屬於愛的答案

作者｜卡羅・波特（Carol Bolt）　　譯者｜念念
責任編輯｜朱紫綾　　美術主編｜藍秀婷　　封面內頁設計｜鄭婷之　　內頁排版｜菩薩蠻數位文化有限公司

發行人｜張輝明　　總編輯｜曾雅青　　發行所｜三采文化股份有限公司
地址｜ 台北市內湖區瑞光路 513 巷 33 號 8 樓
傳訊｜ TEL:8797-1234　FAX:8797-1688　　網址｜ www.suncolor.com.tw
郵政劃撥｜帳號：14319060　　戶名：三采文化股份有限公司
初版發行｜ 2019 年 1 月 31 日　　定價｜ NT$450
　　15刷｜ 2024 年 6 月 15 日